# WHEN WE WERE
# **CHERISHED**

# BOOKS BY EVE SHELNUTT:

Poetry

*First a Long Hesitation*, Carnegie Mellon University Press
*Recital in a Private Home*, Carnegie Mellon University Press
*Air and Salt*, Carnegie Mellon University Press
*When We Were Cherished*, Carnegie Mellon University Press

Fiction

*The Girl, Painted*, Carnegie Mellon University Press
*The Musician*, Black Sparrow Press
*The Formal Voice*, Black Sparrow Press
*Descant*, Palaemon Press
*The Love Child*, Black Sparrow Press
*Sparrow, Sixty-Two*, Black Sparrow Press

On Writing

*The Writing Room: Keys to the Craft of Fiction and Poetry*,
Longstreet Press
*Writing, the Translation of Memory*, Macmillan Publishers, Inc.
*The Magic Pencil: Teaching Children Creative Writing, editions I and
II*, Peachtree Publisher

As Editor

*The Confidence Woman: 26 Female Writers at Work*, Longstreet
Press
*My Poor Elephant: 27 Male Writers at Work*, Longstreet Press

# Advance Praise for
# When We Were Cherished

Written with spare and vivid imagery, in shades of humor and from wells of loss, Shelnutt's poems offer a moving study of love, family, and isolation. Most striking is the humility of perspective, despite the depths the poems probe. *When We Were Cherished* carries the light of language into memory where mystery still darkens the recesses.

—Daniel Lowe
  Professor, Community College of Allegheny County


As does all her work, Eve Shelnutt presents us, first, with that grand shock of recognition. It is a miraculous thing to be able to do that, especially since our initial thought is, "Why didn't I have eyes and ears and heart enough to report and share that?" There is no wasted space between her words, her lines, and so each word and line settles into us with all the more preciousness. And then soon after, there arrives a special splendor that comes from a writer who knows our world ("the ironworks' first spine-twitching sounds" and "our few words remind me of crumbs"). The better writers have an amazing way of somehow blending those worlds, and Ms. Shelnutt does that with all of *When We Were Cherished*. We raise our eyes from her pages and realize, gradually, that we are the better for being in our own world and so appreciative for being able to visit hers. We receive her work humbly, as we should with all great gifts.

—Edward P. Jones
  Winner of The Pulitzer Prize for *The Known World*


These poems spring from a deep consciousness at once sophisticated and primal: an extraordinary collection, combining narrative power with a darkly brilliant vision. Eve Shelnutt writes with a voice for the ages.

—Cary Holladay
  Author of *The Quick-Change Artist: Stories*

At the end the reader can't help but feel that a major experience has taken place in the journey. That's so rare in poetry books these days.

Shelnutt applies the personal intensity one expects of confessionalism to expand beyond it in poems that create so many wonderful characters and situations that the reader can only marvel in surprise and delight. Thoroughly international, with an elegance of style which evokes the individual, local and temporary to transcend them completely, this book shows how experience and hard-won wisdom, far from dulling the emotions, can make them shine with the brilliance of insight.

–John Bensko
   Author of *The Iron City*


In Eve Shelnutt's new volume of poems *When We Were Cherished* we are given the chance to examine the interior and exterior of our being, our relationship with nature and with others. At white heat, and in that place of other, we are carefully introduced to motherhood, wise and affectionate love, and to places we have known for long periods of time, places that have to do with the human heart. These are poems that are rich in vision because their lyricism and rhythms catch and expose the intricacies of a Bach invention while carrying the reader aloft on the melodies of a Chopin Nocturne. These are poems which quietly ask for our attention because they are about enlightenment and illumination.

–Herbert Woodward Martin
   Author of *Inscribing My Name*

# WHEN WE WERE CHERISHED

*By Eve Shelnutt*

Carnegie Mellon University Press
Pittsburgh 2013

# Acknowledgments

Anne Allen, my younger sister, listened by phone to many revisions of the poems in *When We Were Cherished*, having first read them in manuscript form. Her attentiveness was complete and invaluable.

Daniel Lowe read the collection with unusual attention, and I incorporated a number of his particularly acute suggestions into the manuscript.

My son Greg Shelnutt spent hours at my computer gathering the disparate poems. I thank him for his time, but particularly for his deep and abiding integrity, his infectious sense of humor, and his devotion and love, all of which awe, humble, and sustain me.

Finally, my gratitude goes to John Berger, whose *Unto Their Labors* gave seeming flesh to the writing of Franz Fanon. Berger's art criticism and novel *A Painter of Our Time* have deepened my understanding of the visual arts. Berger's book about the country doctor John Sassal evinces Berger's range of empathy and political commitment as he and the photographer Jean Mohr record Sassal's selfless service to the poor and depressed. Berger exemplifies for me how much a writer's life and work can matter.

Book design by James Berndt

Library of Congress Control Number 2012938563
ISBN 978-0-88748-566-4
Copyright © 2013 by Eve Shelnutt
All right reserved
Printed and bound in the United States of America

10  9  8  7  6  5  4  3  2  1

# CONTENTS

*for Anne Justice Allen and Greg Shelnutt*

# TANGO

Some memories are like
invested capital in an old regime
fallen finally into peace. Others
fill us with shame sea-deep, and
those never cease to crest.
Some lodge like a bullet in
the heart as though to prove they
remain jealous: *Oh, Love of my Life,
who am I, with my heart so over-
filled?* Some memories are quite
handsome—tall and lithe, a little
dark, bowing deeply before you,
and you find yourself twirling,
spinning. Your back arches
backwards, your head almost
touches the floor, until suddenly
caught, you are breathless and
filled with joy in your red dress,
three-inch silver heels, your
long hair sweeping the floor.

# GEOGRAPHY

It's all over the world, is it,
in France, in England, in Portugal
(where I found myself one year)
the cabdrivers want to know what

they think is essential: "Where to?"
And only because I like the name, I
said at once, "Pernambuco." Why not,
since I had left a husband not precisely

because he never used guidebooks,
but close enough: those hundreds of
little suffocating habits I began to
enumerate to the judge until she got

the point. Perversions she probably
imagined when interrupting me would
actually have been a relief. . . . But
never mind. I went to Pernambuco on

my sea legs in fond memory, perhaps,
of an on-board drunk. (You see, I trust,
how nothing in the world is innocent.)
As for this town in Brazil: boats

carried the names *Tejo* and *Lima* and
*The Iamega*. And the children, oh,
the ones I noticed as they begged for
coins had ears so beautifully curved

I thought: seashells. Their mothers—
so young! —wore hats lovely as
themselves. What else did I learn
in Pernambuco? That men are as

careless as children. Such a new
thought. . . . Indeed, I recovered there,
although from what mental ailment
I couldn't say, as it was vague as

a memory of an itch. And I returned
home as lonely as I had been before.
Except now and then I remembered the
street children jumping over open

sewage drains. Intense, they were, yet
always laughing, the smallest often
slipping down, torn shorts wet, hands
covered in slime. I learned, I'd say,

how indiscriminate and persistent
joy can be in, at least, Pernambuco.

# NO PLACE FOR YOU, MY LOVE

How we move from Bach to Mexico
Because you suddenly remember the priest
Luis Sandro, his serious donkey Bibiche;

How if you're sick of Munich I ask
What's Vienna like this time of year, and
Where to purchase yellow roses in winter.

How mist like a clumsy animal set free
Swallowed up fences, streams, voices,
Some singing across a window ledge, hymns.

How by the grace of fever, a cone of light
From a pocket torch shone on Kleist's
Feet, then moved upward to his face just

Seconds before he died. How you answered,
"We should take him home," yet stood
With him in your arms a few yards from

Our house, looking up at the sky as he
Slept. How, without knowing why, I spent
That night awake. Or half-awake, for I saw

You stand outside in Saint Peter's snow, the
Square almost deserted, our son below your
Knees in his unsnapped red suit and cap.

# HOW NOT TO FALL IN LOVE

It's complicated, as we now say,
this business of not falling in love.

First you must move to another
state with all your art and books

that have been such good friends
for years; and have a son who,

even though a sculptor, reads!
Meaning he can ship you just

what you want to read now, even
when it's a staggering amount.

And you develop a very slight
case of leukemia, for which naps,

you tell the new neighbors, must
be taken once a day, mostly (this

you do *not* say) when they're
prone to drop in with a gift of

food, or, heaven help us, *Vogue.*
And you stay off the Internet,

which could help you find, oh
goodness, a "Perfect Match."

Food gets delivered if you get it
arranged, fees and smiles and

guile. And stamps, of course,
since you are the old-fashioned one

who still sends out letters; and
small gifts from a mail-order house

or two. Your hair you cut yourself,
a handheld mirror to get back strands

no one will ever notice but you.
And maybe the most pertinent of all,

you revive the image of your un-
requited lover and hold so true

he would be amazed. Or maybe
not, for he has always known in

the first moment of waking, our
arms and legs, as in an old, silent

film, so comically entangled.

# CEREMONY IN WINTER

Two girls walk through rain,
sisters who at home share sly,
meaningful glances when their
parents' arguments begin. How

untouched by tenderness, as
usual. You should hear them!
It is winter, their scalps are numb,
their ungloved fingers sting.

Sleeves of their red sweaters drip,
rain soaking the bottoms of the
paper bags that could easily split.
Each girl senses a panic tighten

her chest. So without warning,
this sudden rush of icy air, and
leaves shredded into brown
clumps underfoot, macadam so

wet they move to the leaf-strewn
grass verges. This rain falls so
steadily their humming has the
lilt of flutes. How lovely to be

home, Mother drying your hair,
Father making coffee, and, for
you, cups of hot chocolate. How
it always is when whatever it was

with them is over.

# DESIRE, AGE TEN

I wanted our house painted red
not for the color I admit would
be too garish for a family mostly
private and in good taste (Heifetz
and Lily Pons, one-sided records
on which Caruso sang like my
father would have sung had he
known the least thing about song).

No, the color itself would have been
scandal and shame, but, Oh, to put
on a brass plate on our door the words
*Casa Rosa*, how that would have
answered all I wanted, when, as it
was, houses we lived in changed
with every year, or less, if the TV
station asked my father," for God's

sake," to do the weather, in which
case we instantly moved on. What
complete luxury, a brass plate I,
alone, would polish. Maybe another
would be attached by our gardener
to the wrought-iron gate. And so,
suddenly, we had a gardener! Named
Alfred-the-Great, who specialized in

roses, and herbs for our cook, named
Lela Greer, who, on her initiative,
hired Charleen to wash the pots and
pans, and, when she was fully trained,
translucent china with gold rims and
goblets of lead crystal. Once, in the
library in Maitland, Florida, I sat

on the floor in the children's room

reading James Jones' huge war novel
hidden behind Roald Dahl's book for
kids and peaches and cream. Yes,
the world *is* often quite nice, especially
just now, when I imagine my friends
from all those dozen towns lined up
(Guinevere first, then Claire) for me
to see again. How novel that would be!

# FEBRUARY 23, 2005, 6:25 P. M.

We drew moth-like to his body
and, still, they called that flame
death, although we beat our
foreheads against his chest,

tears sputtering disbelief until
morning's halo of sun shone
on the three windows. At my
house (his body taken away from

that room we will never forget)
night came with a few strands of
gold that turned matte. Even now
when we imagine our fierce grope

for his life to flare again, we find
on our cheeks tears such as rolled
over his hands when, as children,
we flew to him for healing. And

for this father who was always
leaving: not for pressure on our
cheeks did we go for days un-
washed on our faces, but for

across our foreheads the dust of wings.

# SPRING

Fallen overnight, the snow
is composed for ruin, and birds,
gathering anything even partially
visible, suggest by their flurry
another snow by nightfall. Old
oaks measure the width of limbs
by small hillocks of white in which
squirrels' tiny feet have left pock-
marks, and their tails' sweep: bark
exposed. Hard to imagine squirrels
complicit in what is perishable,
their horde of nuts gathered weeks
ago. Yet those paw-marks could
not be made by bears or dogs.

The daughters yawn: pristine air, the
woods' portal into silence. . . . Where
to sleep this night of what will be
snow's second fall? Their father,
before whose house they stand, had
gone north to die, and died. They turn
away on the stone walk he had laid,
the house key pulled back into one
daughter's gloved palm. The car they
rented is clean-swept, not the snow-
covered iconic shape of "car." The
house *was* his, and now is theirs. Yet

*not*, this afternoon of grief's baptism
in white.

# DONNA'S REVOLUTIONARY NOTES

Inordinately, we must like
the idea of poverty:
climbing stairs to attics;
sleepless nights' marrow
as we hatch vast plans. We

hope to nourish ourselves
on commemorative arts
of our history and its too many
illusions; to honor it in so far
as it explains how our own
mothers and fathers live
happily in such bad faith.

Our flesh, our very hearts:
we are the gloom of which
poets write, and a brute
rejection of man's suffering.

Sometimes we spend whole
evenings in discussion of
erotic subjects simply to
keep ourselves ready to
explode into action.

We allow no one to speak of
dead comrades, a rule some
from distant provinces
find especially painful.
Ours must be painstaking
silence, for giants are alive
within our country and they
thrive on madness, such as
rosewood caskets burnished

in gold-plating. Yours, if your
family insists on caskets,
must be of rough-planed,
untreated, pine wood.

Mine will be a shroud of
wool first woven, then
dyed blue and magenta,
being loomed, as I write,
by weavers in Peru, for we
must always plan for death.

Obviously, all the young
women must be both fecund
and cold-blooded, bearing
children intelligent, lithe,
surefooted, and those not
so blessed will learn to cook.

Should you, through torture,
be rendered useless, never,
ever confess. Pain *will* play
its part for, even among those
who torture, it is given mute
respect. The broken body can
tell the world, "The future
is already ours!" By this hand

I do hereby avow.
And may at any time amend.

# EARLY, IN WALES

In corduroy and flashy tie
far too wide; from a ship
moored in silence, they—
escorts of the semi-worldly—

sweetly take him from the pier,
deposit him among younger
women (waiting): this man
who, having refused to buy

land when it was cheap, has
as few prospects as the girls'
brothers or uncles or, for that
matter, their hundred cousins.

His shoes un-peaceably squeak
the route the girls have been
taught to walk, arms, also
instructed, not crossed over

their high breasts; even their
sighs have become less frequent,
almost slight, although their
mothers may account for such

seductive manners, these women
who knit on benches, among the
gulls' shrieks and shocking
swoops. His seething could find

its outlet here, except it is 1936,
long before I inherited a thing.
So much for bad timing;
so much for his adored body.

# END OF MORNING

Water runs red through the town gutters;
a choir practicing for Sunday's Mass
sends long-held notes over sheep heads
hung by steel hooks at the butcher shop.

Two men cup their hands around the aroma
of coffee spread wide by a draught from the
door where a tooth of light from a hallway is
rose-colored and almost seductive, except

it is just past nine in the morning when the
ironworks' first spine-twitching sounds of
the hammer rounds the corner, where a boy
of five or so tries out his new bike

by riding it around and around the fountain.
So far, four times he has bloodied his knees.
Before the fifth, he flings the bike away and
retakes the wicker basket in his fists. It seems

heavy, but he is a boy who exaggerates, being
only five and with only a grandmother to care.
At the general store the owner hangs a pale
yellow crepe de chine dress on a hanger, in

the open door, a dress far too small for the
passing ladies who, having dreamt their parts
long ago, pass briskly by, playing them.
From a pram, an infant alerts its nurse with

a sharp wail, as though the baby has suddenly
awakened in fright. After lifting the child up,
she holds it while turning in a circle, for now
the little square buzzes: human, animal, insect.

"You see? You see?" pulling the baby down
on one syllable, tossing it up on another. I
could report how the child reacted, except
morning is all rush: So much to hazard

until it's finally dark.

# CAFÉ NIGHTS

It is usually done over the first dinner:
he speaks, she speaks, and the candle
flame bends one way, then another in
such unrealistic divisions of time any
long-married couple would know how
new they are to one another—quaint, they
think, which, no matter the thirty-some
years they have together, makes them
suddenly young and in love again. How
it's catching, almost. Except, as the hours
pass and the old couple has gone home
to the separate beds these soon-to-be
lovers cannot imagine: some of the past
each relates has a taint of shame. And
their faces draw nearer the candle's light:
their shoulders rounded, each history now
clutched closer like a cape, the frayed
lining of which should be concealed.
That's what would bemuse the couple
whose worn bodies seem to themselves
unworthy of revelation, with warmth of
their limbs even less than a candle's
flicker. But watch the newly met man
and woman escape the café: Like
a bird whose keeper removes the cover
from its cage—the latent energy too-long
pent-up causing the bird's feathers to flutter
wildly as the bird's eyes are suddenly
hit by light. So go the lovers toward a
bed, his or hers (now it doesn't matter how
scruffy the sheets). Into a dark that only
seems like sudden light.

# CHILD

In a field of blue, from black
irises, questions poured into my
own eyes of robin's egg blue.
Answers? I had swaddled his
bones in faultless flesh, yet he

wanted so much more, asking
how his toes felt in hands most
familiar with my face or his own
fingers splayed wide or lacing:
you've seen it, wishing perhaps

for your own hands to know such
gleeful touches again. And when
words arrived, when I had learned
little beyond the wonder of birth?
Often I checked his breathing.

His least whimper brought milk
seeping from my breasts, even
the merest touch of water from the
shower, no matter, he slept sated.
How generous my body became!

Then one day it came to me so
suddenly I thought my heart would
break: How gleefully he would
begin to wobble surface to surface
away from me, looking startled.

I knew: Only at my death would
he be so startled by distance again.

# HOOFBEATS OF SUMMER

While walking, I saw a boy of
twelve (I thought), bouncing
his school satchel in the rhythm
of his gait. It was like
coming upon a bend where
river and foliage flow as one.

He ran off through a field of tall
grass toward a horse under a tree.
He turned toward me (I'd felt in-
visible) before reaching out to grab
the horse's mane. His smile was
half-knowledge, half-chagrin in

the yellow prism from which I
looked. He lept! Curved his
body in a single motion so fluid
my breath stopped until his back
straightened. Isn't that sign enough
of wonder, a callow boy like that,

half horse?

# IF FELICITY COMES

If felicity comes to him
in this his eighth year
*will* he know what to do?

Grasses, drought-withered,
come barely to his ankles,
but he would have to invite

his three brothers, of whom
one must be held to his chest.
Another barely wobbles one

object to the next, then he
expects wild clapping, hugs.
So deep in her chest is her

sister's death, his auntie's
tears are silence speaking.
Mornings, the grandmother

sits on a three-legged stool,
her back between the frame
and the open door, a long walk

with her three times daily to
the outhouse, modesty not
something she even considers.

Yet, one day no more likely
than all the others, just before
dawn begins to accumulate heat;

when the baby has not yet cried
for water or pap; when the aunt's
body still blankets the three; and

as the grandmother snores the
rhythms of waiting: This softest
of dawns strikes him as a miracle

he must believe, a fervor new
to him and odd. Rising suddenly
is not at all chore-like, and he

tiptoes outside to the acacia tree
whose branches outshine its
leaves in moon's sliver of light.

Lifting both arms to the lowest
limb, he begins swinging his
body back and forth, happier

than all he had dreamt. Ah. . . .
He had thought what to do.

# IN KOGOSHIMA

*–in honor of Ira Zook*

With a conductor's wand
he kept time: such was

my knowledge until,
gesturing, he showed me

rituals far more intricate
than any childlike dream

or the scent of mayhem,
even sorrow hidden in

the moon's travel into
thinning light. He had

crossed an ocean, narrow
straights, rivers

simply to rest on feet
tucked under, back stiff,

mat centered on a pale
bamboo floor—not

waiting, exactly (pleasure
already in his face) for

the ritual service of tea.
Rather, owning the hand

aware, precisely, of how
the cup is to be received,

he did not think, no more
than blossoms could be

said to think. And desire
was never an undertow:

he prepared himself to be
known, and he knew me.

# EXILE OF IMAGINATION

His novels presage misfortune
hot, crackling, poisonous, as if
a mad dog seizes a pen: No

carnality so sordid it would
not do for Georgette or Helena
in grimy rooms with the current

man collapsed in ardors of sleep,
bed narrow, sheet bloodstained
since virgins always sell, though

he, personally, would much prefer
sluts after his wife left with their
two kids in the Audi paid for,

no less, by the virgins' certain appeal.
Naturally, he feels put upon, sitting
on a straight wooden chair before

the ancient computer she left him
when dividing the family goods: the
sterling silver for her and their two

lovely girls who believe, so
far, that he works for Reuter's
from a one-bedroom apartment

no less. . . . And, if he's not careful,
an Italian uncle sits drowsy under
a linden tree, willows bank side the

meandering river he can—Yes!—
actually hear if he stops for a cigarette
(off-brand: *Niagara* or something).

But the alimony, shit, (etcetera),
comes due in a week. Thus sweet
Angelina lets some dude open her

frilly blouse, but *no way* can he
"see" Roderick fresh, Never-mind:
Roderick gets inspired and drags

Angelina on a picnic by a babbling
stream where, under a willow,
he unbuttons her blouse. Ah ha!

She wears no bra. Perfecto! Then,
thinking, he scrolls back. Suddenly
the blouse is white, starched cotton,

ironed as only he can.

# IN THE BREEZE OUR MOTHER MAKES

**1.**

I have two sisters a little sad
and a twin brother at birth
untwining himself from me
in the white cotton of death.

And music in my mother's walk
through such incomprehensible
hope we call him "Father,"
sometimes "That jerk," for our

feelings blow hither and yon
in the breeze our mother makes.

**2.**

In the breeze our mother makes
a house appears on a hill,
a white frame house, two leaning
pines, a dog asleep under one.

And fleas asleep on the back
of the dog docile in outrageous
heat. Inside the stuffy house
we sleep and fail to dream,

awaken late and stretch ourselves
out. Time? Time? The clock
says ten, my sisters' minds
say, "*Not again.*" And soon, we

hear Mother putting on her shoes.

**3.**

I can almost hear her count us out
like beads. Why? In order to
forget we're here, our presence
like a box snapped shut.

She dreams awake, she moves,
she sings, nonsensical songs'
Italian. For Father's gone again,
the jerk. And still she sings.

The roof rises in the sun,
we lift the roof by walking out.
It's emptied ink into our nests
of books. Sometimes it rains

rhythms of my sisters' tears.
Still in rain our mother walks.

She walks in rain, her hair
strings down. Inside, she
dries while whistling. We
adjust, we dress, as she, in white.

**4.**

We feel excited, just a little
sick. His letters come or
fail to come. He's "There"
somewhere shedding skin.

Will we know him 20 years
from now? Mother yawns.
Under the pine our dog
rolls over in the sun.

Red fur glossed by sun,
the glossing ribbons. They
cry, my sisters cry. Mother
says, "Poor souls." Oh,

a double funeral of words.
Dear Father, I did not know
how my mother knew you,
years I wouldn't know,

lacking the body knowing.

**5.**

She sang away, songs
preached the efficacy of
song. Time: looking for
lost sheep with blinded eyes.

A soft perfume of violence.

Have these sisters never
combed the abundant tresses
of an evening? Sadness
in their eyes behold all things.

They're worth too much!

# HOW HE AND I HAVE LOVED

It is a fifth and nameless season,
neither winter, for it warms us;
nor spring, for we plant nothing;
nor fall with the harvest of apples.

Summer seems likely, yet I have neither
bared my legs nor gone sleeveless.
It is a season seemingly endless until
we each die in our time zones so

different we could name the states,
number the differing routes that
would themselves change all the
states we would have named. But

why call it a season at all, in which
wild horses' muffled pawing and
brute snorts suggest they at least are
bored by what never happens. But it

has. Its orbit cannot be slowed by
any astrologist's numbers and charts,
nor the least nod of our heads. Do not
stars flung beyond man's naked sight

still emit light?

# BEFORE THE BIOGRAPHY

I got a cat one day,
beautifully striped,
with a fat, fluffy tail
brown, russet, gold.

All requisite vaccinations
I had it given, and a quite
nice red collar to which
I attached a bell.

And since I was giving
her the wide outdoors,
it was rewarding to hear
its twilight jingles.

"Yerma," I named her,
only that one name even
entered my mind. For
weeks and weeks she was

a most satisfactory pet
approved of even by friends
and relatives who favored
dogs, "essentially," added

a few, which Yerma and I
thought was most polite.
Then, inexplicably, one
bright day in the park, with

Yerma trailing along behind,
I gave her away, just like that.
But the boy's eyes were so
bright, the mother's smile so

dazzling, the two living in a
house, I imagined, in which
kittens would be welcome,
if it came to that. Even the

name I gave away.
Walking home alone, I felt
my solitude more than usual,
that's true, but with great

industry I vacuumed the rugs,
upholstery and, after several
months, began to wear black
again. Did I want Yerma back?

I had not written down the boy's
name, his mother's address,
only supplied a vet's name,
to whom I supposed I could

apply in mercy should loneliness
seem unbearable. Time passed.
Alas, it has always been like that
between me and García Lorca.

And I have never known why.

# INTRUSION AND LIGHT

Well, naturally, just when I want to say
how true, how lovely is my younger sister's
oil painting of several sheep and lambs,

there come our parents arguing inside the
house despite their having died long ago.
Not one of us three would ever say they

let us down when pairing love with fury,
nor doubt our mother's wish to "save" the
future painter from so many brutal words.

As instructed, we took her out to grass or
dirt and had her dig a hole, sit squatting
above it cackling, then watched her cry

when no eggs appeared. And proving,
I suppose, how right our mother had been,
Anne's brushstrokes of lush yet subtle

color make me want to stroke a lamb's
head, its mother's sunstruck back, a lone
tree's mottled bark half-umber in sun.

# LATE NOVEMBER 2011

In a suburban driveway in Silver Spring
a car turns slowly beside a house on a
day unusually warm and full of sunshine.

Gently closing the car door, the man
pats the front hood almost playfully
before opening slowly the opposite door,

then leans over to glide from the seat
a woman holding a baby wrapped in
pink blankets. No cloud in the sky on

this day that the runner, emerging from
a house several miles away, will, alas,
never particularly remember as, in his

new running shoes, he warms up, and,
as the couple enters their front door,
begins his daily run: miles to the capitol.

How fast he is rounding the dozens of
statues along his route, slowing only, as
he always does, just before the Wall and

its slight decline where, also by habit, just
as the incline ends, he glances up to the
name he has "adopted," as he told

his wife after a bitter quarrel; he, at least, is
"essentially" happy, she need not worry,
although they remain, and shall, without

children. He is disappointed, but a kind
of half-life, he thinks, as he bursts into
sunlight again, he has given the soldier,

whose family he imagines now around
a laden table. Inside the house, the new
mother nurses the girl beloved so

fully already it will carry her through
a long life. And, inexplicably (he thinks),
suddenly the runner stops, spins among

the monuments, thinking to himself
how truly fine the day is.

# INTIMACY

Finally the shepherds resettle on
    their linen hems: small

islands of white nailed by a star's
    cold, persistent illumination.

Yet they know themselves stunned as
    their sheep's odor and sounds of

chewing loosen from God's care,
    His sharp flight of relief like

remembering a word you need.
    What else was suddenly absent?

They know goodness is a burro
    laden with silver, and their only

hold on it a frayed rope. Scattering
    again, each hums to himself now

and then to stave off sleep's metro-
    nome of easy breathing. Their

excitement having affirmed the birth of a
    a convincing child, how soothing:

prayers to someone a mother has touched.

# LESSONS

Only yesterday, she played
the violin with her eyes closed.

(I like beginnings that festoon
a story with questions, such as:

Why is she not playing today and
would she do so tomorrow when,

most likely, sorrow will have all
of us reeling?) By then, morning,

her face will be puffy, with many
scratches from his pushing her

into the privet hedge. What would
it be like then for Father, while

driving? Had he not called his two
oldest girls together before the

mantel whose mirror captured
our three faces, two anxious,

and told us, "Your mother has said
she will hang herself if I leave,

so I thought I'd tell you, before I
leave"? True, I did race for weeks

from school bus to house, my chest
exploding, to learn how tiny was

my need: Yes or no? (Good training
for later life, I found, although I

do think an amendment to the adage
about families is needed: Some are

dramatic, some quite boring.) So:
our mother went on for many years.

And we learned to love Father too.

# HUNTERS, GATHERERS

Apparently limitless between 8 & noon,
the carloads of shoppers in which the
talk is always with purpose and scent:

the collected, coveted Wedgewood china
or handpainted ducks. But what of the
diary found tucked behind two Bibles

in which, in 1934, Claudine had knelt
before a priest in Lima, suddenly very
ashamed of the freckles on her hands.

Then—goodness!—only four months
later, she's seduced a vicar in Lyon, and
all at once you're vigorously ashamed,

when what you're seeking is ancient
first edition books, above voyeurism,
truly, yet there is a pile of crepe night-

gowns and heeled bedroom slippers with
fluffy balls in pink. Is that woman who
collects the money—surely not—the

daughter? Is the man of the 8-by-10
couple on the mantel the faithful one
who helped provide for seven children

also framed in gold? How terrible, this
sale of what was once so dear. Believe
me, just after noon in a lilac bedroom,
the world is coming to an end.

# LITERALLY

Not only to some precocious intellectual
such as Genet who, wrongly named a thief,
became one, does it happen, although what
is, is rarely what it seems: the woman, for

example, who sells lemons in the square,
those precise pyramids you, the customer,
must not yourself touch. Only she, from a
box set below the table, assembles your

four or five, thick skins or thin, she decides,
yet how fragrant they are, just so pliable
and no more. You carry them away with
their tartness already in your mouth. As

for her trade, it is not a simple story,
not at all. Alas, she had been spurned,
around age sixteen, when it truly hurts,
by a mangy boy who called her a name

one day after she hopped down from the
crossbar of his bike, then added: "You
are such a shit, you know?" for he had,
of course, an Italian boy's machismo.

So upping even that, he said to her
retreating back, "You are such a *lemon*,"
quite a sting to her developing pride, so
instantly like a cut from a kitchen knife.

She did in the interim all the usual stuff
girls did in those days, got pregnant, in
other words, and married him, upon which
followed a brood of seven, just one more

than they had wanted, which was usual too,
but really too many, needing her tongue
civil for domestic mayhem, what with her
husband working a bit, then off to the café.

Her vocabulary became not the least crude,
although she ended up talking faster than
even the typical Italian and sounding like
an untouchable pyramid of language on the

verge of toppling. But golden, too, if you
took its rhythms into account. The kids
mostly ignored it after each turned old enough
to find himself transport apart from her hip.

But listen to her on Saturdays, after
stalls have sold out and dismantling begins.
That's what gets to her: metal roof struts
often collapsing at once instead of in parts,

the usual dust-black pigeons underfoot, as
well as a few feral cats with their tails held
defiantly high, and a woman in the next stall
who won't let her hair go pepper and salt.

*Then* the lemon vendor lets loose quite a few
perfectly articulated curses at fate, one a
stream almost jaunty when two empty crates
fall on a sandaled foot. It's all a bit much,

Life, that is, until she's home cooking
baked chicken with lemons inside, for that
is always pleasing. Then after the kitchen's
been cleaned, after she's pressed a two-

piece dress for Sunday, she opens the bottle
of Lemonella she and her sons put up and
manages to get far more than woozy, about
which she will have to confess before Mass.

Father: Why did God give me lemons?

# IN THE MUSEUM OF THE IMAGINATION

She lifts one hand silently,
closes the guard's eyes.
All physical consolation begins
ahead of her, perhaps by miles.

To inch forward, crowded by
breath floating in the air with the
least step. All through what
feels like porous bone. And an

unaccountable fear of line,
as though they are little relics.
That frayed, straw hat, those
little white shoes: almost an

eccentricity of the mind now
(at this hour of absent clocks)
regarding her seeming destination
west through open doors.

This afternoon of girl, of lilacs,
of fewer questions of death:
the artists having taken care
in unmuddied strokes, color,

intention in every breath taken
in, pushed out. How simple
this art of imagination is. She
opens the guards' eyes. He lives!

# LITTLE SISTERS OF THE POOR

One miniscule week after she'd arrived:
great commotion in the yard, house, chapel,
the girls' bodies scrubbed by rough brushes,
green soap, kerosene in their lovely hair,
and the nuns combing for hours, clutching
black combs with tiny teeth. All of it
a failure—soon the girls were on low
stools watching hair of all colors fall
around them.

And of course they whimpered under
trees, shivered when their cloth dolls
got swept into black plastic bags, the
girls themselves dragging them out to
the monster bins in the alley. So,
naturally, practical jokes on their keepers
increased like a contagion of sly smiles.

Angelica—can you believe it?—the nuns
named her. And, oh, she was worse, even,
than Fleur, who thieved toffees and licorice
from Mother Beatrice's bowl, smiling
at her with blackened teeth, with blacker
looks taking punishment without tears.

"Let's just face it," said Angelica, "they're
bored," the words becoming a kind of
litany recited after lights-out snickers
and tears and plans for revenge "with more
teeth in it." (Angelica's contribution, the
sort brought in from the outside world.)
"God help us," said the visiting abbess,
"should she ever discover Baudelaire."
Just one of those mysterious things, the

nuns decided, the abbess often said.

When finally the school year ended,
Angelica was passed on without the grades
to back it up. You can find her in any
Woolworths, behind the handkerchief
counter, chewing gum and sulking. Until,
that is, you see her one fine spring day,
out in the town park, pushing a pram.

It is an old story of Angelicas everywhere,
how they stay lovely longer than most
women, how, if you meet their men in
a sporting goods store, they seem happy.
How life is so often beautiful and unfair.

# IN PLACE OF SOMEONE ELSE

Mist rose the whole time we were on the river.
It cast a white haze on the rowboat, over
young willows, the brambles grown
twisted through trees' watery offshoots and
short clusters of wild oak. I noticed all this
as his right arm flung out again and again
toward fish he imagined waited in the water.

I read both the color of the sky and his body
as confluence I had not yet known in my life.
Then, suddenly, I could think only of the boat,
of paintings of women I had seen in museums:
women who leaned back luxuriously. How,
having gone hatless in sunlight, their eyes
burned until it seemed time itself had rowed away.

It did not hurt more to know: in the nature of a sluice
he would soon leave me. "Only a little farther,"
he said, his tact ingrained. Words have always
come to me late, as though I must first gather,
like a bundle of dry kindling, many images
before striking the match. *I did not like either
of us that day, no matter how fresh the fish*

*you would take home for your wife to cook.*

# PADDING OF SHEEP'S WOOL

During the first cold spell of winter
the retired shepherds stay abed, half
sideways, half flat, none, for aches,
placed more advantageously than the

others, all their bones together adding
up to pain, like a prison sentence for
having done nothing but tend sheep,
about which they think, although not

together, at once, maneuvering the
steppes of sleep that seem often like
a hillside whose contours go on, on,
traveling through the valley where

both sheep and shepherds have lived
almost unbothered until now. And it
has always been difficult when winter
comes downing fences, rain-to-snow

to brief respites of sun that can often
confuse both sheep and men, until
only the seasons of shearing and
lambing are in the air to anticipate.

But the old men hardly talk, since in
the field you can feel slightly mad
talking to sheep, and the dog simply
cannot be coddled lest he forget his

job, the one pat on the back enough
to keep him alert and proud. But I
meant to write about what the men
wear to bed. Except you can guess.

Oh, do not take it for granted:
wool is probably more precious
than you've imagined, for, as the
shepherds turn in their beds, you can

sense, no matter the woolens they
invariably wear, that winter *does* come
for them, if not for the sheep both
white and black in coats so thick, so

curled, it is almost like a dream.

# SOPRANO

After mild forgetting:
another's lover hums
rhythmically close.
I must see him, I must
listen. Or somehow
have brothers, sameness
a chorale wherein origins
defy the score. Maybe

my arms direct a hall
of sight-readers
interpreting what they
can until the solo one
dares sing, her mouth
composed for sound
then the sound itself.
Its lilt the beloved once

found so lovely. Who the
vessel is.

# THE AUNTS YEARN

Should they find men who
like foreheads high much
as one looks with favor on
mountains free of snow;

if these few men whose
former wives (not very
conveniently divorced)
have sired children (so

conveniently grown and
gone away); if the dapper
gentlemen remember words
sounding almost arcane,

thus reassuring in the way
of men who speak past
pipes unlit, then stow in
jacket pockets of wide

wale corduroy? If, if. . . .
The aunts entertain on
porches or beside manned
fires in parlor grates.

It is as it should be: restive
women on brocade chairs,
just so. Across from them
perch the suitors, only some-

what abashed. Were they
ever caldrons of desire?
Consider how little silver
rests in cutlery drawers;

how many days of eating
it takes to make a dish-
washer full; and in the
often inclement weather

three minutes sweep clean
a clothesline on which hang
no plaid shirts of flannel
with left pockets torn or

pinstripes whose white
collars require bleach,
so touchy, the inner
yellow grime. Yes, yes.

all remembered until sun
pours forth. Still, what
utter boredom, such
thankless chores! Except:

skirt-smart, with banners—
*Down With Twin Sheets—*
*Down With Single Pillows—*
here they are, passing drinks:

the ageless aunts a-fever.

# CASUALTIES, 1945

Mornings, more than after dark,
she began to tremble:

having given himself to her,
he could be ordered away.

Yet, he bought a canoe
equipped with paddles.

Sun baked the tile roof,
white shutters kept at bay

heat, except theirs, doubled
when making love. And

facts, so terribly real, so grim
during war. "*Whose*," he asked,

*was* she before he entered her life?
But she would never say,

laughing instead because her
heart was full. The uniform,

perfectly creased, was the color
of applesauce she made herself.

Bread, before being toasted,
the bite of his lovely teeth.

But to shorten a story lasting
as long as each drew breath:

he served abroad, then returned,
he and she both more and less

than they had been before.

# LONE VIEWER OF A FILM

When he had emptied his plate
twice, then shoved it aside

he stood in the vast room with
an arm extended as though

to rest a hand on her shoulder.
From a distant perspective the

gesture could seem natural,
from a foreign film where

attention must never waiver:
a basket of bread on a white

cloth, the sound of raw silk
a-shiver against white sheets,

her throat long, exposed; the
room full of white blossoms.

Which idea came first: husband
hesitantly eating an apple or

wife who says she never dreams?
The credits roll as the husband

slings the core from a window
where winter is clearly visible.

Yet some mistake has occurred,
for now sunlight pours through

the sweeping sleeves of her
blouse. How very French, those

enigmatic endings! She will doze
all afternoon, he thinks, mouth open.

When she awakens, her smudged
lips feel dry. Of course, he, who

has watched her for so long, never
ever would see her suffer, and

brings water. It may be a new
ending; who's to know since,

after all, he was busy eating. And
for that small matter, since life is

most often revision: Why not a
flute of champagne? She is quite

beautiful, to which the husband,
poor sap, has grown accustomed.

So: the best champagne! The very
best, except, for the moment, its

name escapes him, nibbles but won't
be caught. . . . Ah yes, how it is when

you're older. Then you sleep on it,
and those dreams are not bad, not

half bad at all.

# BRYAN, OKLAHOMA

Crouched in a field of scattered bushes
a dog in a shaggy, red jacket of fur,

and many (I imagine) memories of
once-scented prey, its nose quivering,

then its legs suddenly in motion, and
from a distance he seems more like a

low-slung Porsche at top speed, until
with its neck hair raised, it barks wildly

at some gopher beneath the sandy
surface, barks without cessation until

the gopher sticks its head out so quickly
I wonder at what I have seen. Which

of these wild creatures (for the dog *is*
wild and, for that, frightening) won that

skirmish among blowing tumbleweed
under a scorching sun so bright I turn

away? Soon the sky would smell
briefly of iodine before lightning flashed

jagged across the expanse. What
sky would the stars after dusk attend?

Now, to furious barking, I look back
across the expanse of scrub to see the

red dog racing toward me with what
looks like its whelp in its mouth smeared

with blood. I step back in horror, for now
the dog loosens its jaws to drop the gopher

at my feet. Have you received such a gift,
the dog panting on a little dune with a

satisfied stare into your eyes, your hands
refusing to pat its head? And feeling guilt?

# YOUNG LADIES STANDING
# ABOVE A WATERFALL

The photographer liked to snap
images of fear, since he had
no developed sense of danger,
his finger so constantly on the
shutter he forgot to notice his

feet, just as the young women
whose center of balance, quite
different one from another,
must have seemed for a brief
moment irrelevant. A high

fall of water is about sound,
the icy spray, the peering down
from such a height in awe's
displacement from fear itself.

Who slipped first was not
recorded, or was, and the camera
never found. Nor how many
the ladies until late at night
when those who housed them

found news cameras flash awake
their grief in front of policemen
with bowed heads and flashlights
held respectfully down. The

fathers, the mothers, all manner
of kin, some too small to stand,
did not grieve over the white
bodies until late morning, in
the morgue with flourescent
lighting, rows of green sheets.

They beheld mornings there-
after with detachment, like
those for whom steadiness is
the anodyne for every impulse.

The town held citizens of
anti-quickness, a sort of cult,
for no one (had life not said?)
could ever be quick enough.
*Adelaide, Louisa, Florence,*
*Betsy, Evelyn, and Iris. . . .*

And the man with the "classy" Nikon
(it was said) named Ray Bledsoe,
whose grandmother, with whom
he lived, remembered exactly what
he ate for breakfast; that he had put
an extra lens, for distances, in his
camera bag. But did he use it?

Ray Bledsoe, from then on, was
always spoken of by his first and
last names. In time, the "ladies"
became "the girls." And in the

hearts of those who could never
satisfy grief, "the girls" are in
perpetual free-fall, yet far, far away,
like shadows held between thumb
and the finger that points.

# THE WAKE

The woman who is motionless
has neither bed nor grave, only

a wooden table around which
the grief-struck family gathers,

touching her hands and quickly
drawing back, looking shamed by

how suddenly cold she has become.
If, among the living, we distribute

the wounds of her death, what about
the children to whom she had shown

such tenderness? Outside now, they
play with whatever they can find and

broadcast their squeals, sorrow
hidden behind their usual joy.

When it comes to them again as their
mother draws the blankets close, they

begin suddenly to cry. Outside, a
cloud moves away from the moon as

if to console anyone wise enough to
look. But these children depend on

their mother's face, and now are
wordlessly afraid. It was their grand-

mother who has died. The mother's
face can never be as consoling again.

# SITES AMONG FAMILY

Three flowers in a clear vase;
a saddled horse outside that

carried a cousin. Guests, all kin
around an oak table, sanded,

smoothed, waxed by my mother
until it gleams in the windows'

light on a Sunday at noon. One
at the table holds up a single

glove, raising an already arched
eyebrow. It alone says "my

older sister." Outside an unseen
beehive, the Queen too hidden

as always by her drones; an image
of my mother in the gatherer's

headdress pulling out a comb.
Olga, the youngest cousin, licks

her fingers, a blue napkin
ignored beside her plate.

Nine mouths move up, down,
the male cousins' Adams' apples

appear large when they swallow.
Suddenly Cynthia spots something,

rises, then returns to the table with
one white glove as Anne, the "baby"

of my parents' three, looks at me
anxiously, as though we had a pact.

If this were about sound, I might
have asked my father, Why do you

grind your teeth all night? And for
my mother the question she most

dreads: Do we all have souls that
will go to heaven? But my cousin's

horse he neglected to tether arrives
suddenly at the screen door. Now

we all open our mouths wide, showing
teeth and tongues and bits of food.

Soon Mother clears the table of plates.
And if you imagine that I simply

forgot to mention our heads bowed
for the foods' blessing before we ate:

we did not say a blessing, knowing
ourselves, gathered, blessing enough,

like gloves found wholly sufficient
for church or funerals or weddings.

One for each hand, preferably a pair
that fits, each matching the other.

# MODESTY

I wanted to be a woman who scrubbed tables.
I wanted my woes hooked among worn pans.
Coming to desire at fifteen in the storehouse

hurt like a job I liked least among many others.
The keeper of the keys would know almost
at once how my drying my tears meant I

could carry trays without giving the child away.
I wanted a blouse with ties opening quickly,
less for the man who would soon discard me

than for a child whose beauty would not be his
or mine, for beauty is its own empire and as
imperious and lonely as his. When I laughed,

often, since you asked, I noticed how I earned
an honored place among the other women,
how even the calmest folding of linen became

somehow a mute rebellion against his whims.
How utterly ridiculous, falling on my knees
while smiling that little smile he loves, when,

of course, I wish him dead.

# PAPER DOOR

Behind it, a few figures ghostly-by-design
murmur as softly as breezes lift a baby's hair,

words frivolous or fierce as bee sting, discrete,
perhaps, as in place names on a reliable map:

If you follow, you shall arrive, impatience
tame as feathers on a woman's hat. And

sight is pruned until any passerby may only
guess what depth of passion sways the guests.

If swept in oil across a gesso underlay, they
would appear less Mondrian yet more than Klee.

If the figures were, say, birds: one wing of each
is wet, yet seeks to lift (and would, one senses,

fail). Like that, exactly so, the sisters, close and
quite expressive, ask their parents now deceased:

"What kind of feeling is what we feel? Why have
we never felt it before, how long does it last?"

What they need is nectar (small sips at first such as
one gives to the starving) of apples and blueberries,

cherries, peaches, oranges, strawberries, plums.
This will keep the sisters healthy for a long

period of throat-parching grief. This, believe me,
is what they want: it seems so true to nature.

# PROVIDENCE

This could be the story of twins
carried in the wheels' whine of

a cart over asphalt twice, a
mother unable to say where she

hurt if not all over and forever.
Except the girl kept breathing.

Thus nature unfolding each day
reminds the mother how a dog's

bark echoes from hills, how one
leaf falling in autumn suggests

the next will also fall. And how
a mother can be placed in some

awful town as the father roams,
no watchful shepherd, he. Who

provides? The girl on a bicycle,
of course, who brings her mother

violets, daffodils, even peonies
stolen from the widow's yard.

Oh to be good for something, as
you listen for your father's car.

And on days of sea squall, skin's
taste of salt, your homeward

brother's tattered breathing.

# THE DISTANCES

I saw a man
gorgeous and lithe.

How to look:
if he's someone I should

know, naively at
home at century's end.

He will sing,
hands clenched behind his

neck, a pose his
body likes and thus repeats.

To see him
loving his body so much:

the same cannot
happen to just anyone.

Thinking hard, I
ask, What? Is he just one

of Jim Dine's
wry, yet morose birds?

All right, I admit
I'm completely alone, ambling

without touching
more than accidental shoulders,

that boy with his new
eyeglasses just before eight

when his teacher
calls him to a huge map. . . .

Forget indoors:
I am now crossing a wooden

bridge as river's
ice breaks into chunks, and

next to my feet, four
bluish~what? Let nature decide!

Now look:
there he is again, that man with

a brown fedora.
I mean, I can always and forever

imagine love,
continue leaning forward until

I see rivulets
rush madly over the river stones.

# THE GLASS BETWEEN THEM

Her forehead against the window,
she watched her father cry, as if

their few minutes under the same roof
had been a spell's destination and

meant something was finished: a
secret shaking wet leaves over his head,

she merely a camera lens suddenly
given consent, himself broken off

and pliant. Had he not always worn
hand-tailored clothes; his voice, his

gestures tailored by him in countless
hours willing perfection, meaning

without an identifiable place? Did
he cry against his attainments? And

how would she ever know without
learning sorrow's incredible zeal?

# ARCHAEOLOGY

Before my husband came home,
we walked through woods from a
swimming pool's cold water, our
shoulders touching as we talked.

Near the house, seeing him outside,
you asked, "Will you be all right?"
How bitterly I laughed, while saying,
"Oh yes." Every sound I made

those days had its distinct pain
seeking a way out. It was not
exactly untrue: I *did* love him,
if the body thrusting upward

through deep water as a precise
amount of air seeped from lungs
tight and ignorant of how far
above the surface lies, is proof.

Then one brilliant day in summer
I gave up that particular pain
when noticing leaves offered
archways of green. You and I

of course went on talking, the
particular words insignificant,
so tenderly did we breathe into
the telephone seasons of breath.

I've read that natives sometimes
unearthed male bones nestled near
a female's. And I think: silence
must always come with such a

find, intimacy, what we want most
to unearth. Now I've come across
pictures of ourselves, alone, we've
sent each other over time, asking:

What fate kept these two apart?

# SHAKEN

Pity the two women
their brace of doves.

Staring wide-eyed,
they shiver. (Cooing

spares you nothing,
would continue unheard.)

And the vision, saying it
softly: the selling of

doves! It makes one feel
strange. Yet winters come,

their varnished leaves of
homely white. Patiently

the women say it: What
they want is money. At

last I did believe them and,
having paid, then received,

released its body, hands
held high. It returned to

one woman's basket. What
I believe *should* happen

is often like that dove.

# BETWEEN MIND AND FLESH

Nurse in her starched white:
"You hardly suffered," as if,

even as he wailed self-welcome
to the world of bright lights,

I would need a much deeper pain
than those his birth had inflicted

in order to own him whom I
would never own, his very name

as he lay beating his heels on my
chest a mere first installment of

what else I now owed the world.
Had I, when he was so safely

inside me, considered fully what
relinquishment meant? At water's

least touch when I showered,
milk flowed from my breasts

as he slept sated by milk.
Once, before we went outside,

I wrote *snow* across a window.
In it, we opened our mouths,

laughing at snow. One day of
its constant fall, we lay flat on

a drift in our padded clothes,
dark blue on white. I imagined

how we would look if seen from
a great height. I spread my arms,

flapping them across the snow
to show him how. I almost said

*"Angels"*, then caught myself at once.
To my son, I would never lie.

# CASE X

A cold omelet and two aspirin,
a black dog, barking, that
trotted away through rain:

Isn't that how it was, Francesca,
when he wasn't marrying you?
Animal-like in deft movement

across the bed, and all night
his body playing yours like
a wind harp, obsession's ice

melting at dawn, Francesca?
And the ache between your legs
brushed away like a sodden cat

that returns like a whim you're due:
Weren't you shivering in the livery
of sex? Seized, then sobbing?

You had, if we're not mistaken,
a few splendid nights when you
did not seem like a girl at all

and he smelled of dew. Which
should have defeated the virulent
misery of You, isn't that so, our

Most Beautiful Francesca?

# THE HUSBAND, YEAR EIGHT

Her name on my lips is often
burnt sugar. Then an acrid

silence in which I want to go
away, then come home again:

an artist who leaves a painting
in order to see it anew tomorrow,

his last brushstroke suggesting
a thick swirl into light. If I close

one eye I can see her brushing her
teeth to remove a bitter taste.

Our son, still asleep, seems almost
inconceivable, and yet, mornings,

three ladder back chairs sit before
windows' unpredictable hue of

winter's sunlight. We talk not
with each other, but with our son.

Must this "Portrait of a Marriage"
be unhooked from the easel, rolled

into a cylinder of color bleeding
one into another? Sometimes

I imagine her in new dresses,
legs across an unfamiliar sofa.

I even seem to hear another man's
low murmur in her ear when we sit

watching the evening news. Her
power over me then is quite clear.

When we ceased to discuss our son
we let hope go. And I fear, above

everything I fear, his going one day
into the attic, age sixteen or so,

and opening boxes of ornaments
we fastened onto fresh trees from

his grandfather's farm. I *am* warned.

# LIVE BIRTH

Bred deep in the ocean of my
mother's body (left expelling
the fleshless spine of my twin
floating leagues deep to the sea's
floor), I arrived on shore through
cresting foam, specks of sand,
and, standing, thought the world
empty, awaiting me. Yet, turning,
I saw the Others' houses where,
after being invited in, I saw relics
from Time they must have deemed
most precious: the cracked blue
vase filled with dried flowers; and
seemingly old photographs in which
few smiled: a veritable orchard of
faces, while, in the orchard itself,
apples decayed under trees. A man
suggesting a wish to be examined
more deeply brewed coffee in a
charred pot as a lamp sputtered
white trails of smoke against the
blind of a window. Notice how my
vocabulary grew! Yet: to what
keening pitch do the wounded listen?

I waited an achingly long time until,
as though it were my brother's gift,
I heard myself say *I love you*, quickly,
urgently. When he smiled, I thought:
He's remembered the sea's occasional
phosphorescence, bringing light.

# WATERS

Poor cats
disporting their tails like flags
behind lace curtains, most windows
closed until afternoon grows cooler
falling into the hammock of night.

Linea, my sister, off in the fevered
city of Miami although she may
try Boston instead, where rumor
has it the pay is better. Except there
it's so terribly cold, with snow!

Families in this latitude at dinner,
just like us, when the sea, as we sit,
moves as it's most often portrayed
in movies; that is, deceptively calm.

In China—think of it—the boats are
tiny, the men's lives so precarious
their wives carry prayer beads openly
as the youngest son peers out from
shores so veiled in fog he keeps it
secret, like a kind of prayer.

But, still, there's Linea, actually the
family favorite, which I don't mind,
washing her face in Miami (I've decided).
To the basinful, she's no doubt added
rosewater for her underarms, and
I insist, *is* washing her face. Who

in Miami will kiss her and what if he
has a terrible cold? I mean, that note
she squeezed into my palm at the air-

port saying, "I'll find him," surely was
not about Papa, given our mother dyed
her hair red and got monstrously fat.

Remember how Linea said at age
eleven she'd tell me everything when
she turned twelve? She didn't. Which
is just like sisters who get all the goods.
Let's see: Perfumed water in the
basin, her sputtering over and over as

her sleeves get wet. Never, ever, I bet
will we hear from Linea again.

# AGAINST OPERA

1.
Spent after making love,
panting as our breathing
masters itself, now we

sit side by side against the
wood headboard, blankets
pulled to our chins, perhaps

wondering which of us will
go make coffee, warm the
brioche, bring it all on a tray.

2.
Tart smell of our bodies, their
residual heat in damp sheets
crumpled into waves, a muted

oratory of wind under eaves
reeking of such leaf decay we
could imagine several murders

have happened nearby, of, say,
spouses, who in fact are home
waiting to be mesmerized by

what lies we'll invent this time
from the worlds within us of
which so much remains unknown.

3.
Nor do we interest Death at all.

# A FORMER ORPHAN TRAVELS

Some mouths of his bus-mates hang
half open where metal of cheap
dentistry shows the sites of slight but,
he imagines, perpetual, residual aches.

His own tongue feels around a tooth,
right, lower, back, so suggestive is
his thought suddenly released into a
world larger than he's ever seen. It's

all a bit unnerving, in fact, yet he
supposes it's all about money that he
lacks. In a small town (as far as this
Greyhound goes), he comes upon a

café where he orders what he figures
he can afford: a cup of black coffee
to which he adds three packets of
brown sugar such as he's not seen in

the place he mentally named "before."
And stirring and stirring with a metal
spoon (a kind of music to accompany
Patsy Cline) he suddenly announces to

anyone among the row who cares to
listen (laughing a bit to make it all
right so early in the morning): "I'm
a orphan," which causes the waitress

doubling as the cook to turn with a
spatula in hand to ask (and, really,
it's an insult), "Honey, aren't we
all orphans in the end?"

# JOURNEY BY TRAIN

1.
To take from your bag a long Russian novel
is to approve the other travelers' silence
tinged by minor problems, such as whether
the aunt will have received news of Uncle's

defection with a shrug or grand fury, this
Cheshire-cat curiosity they would share
if their children were not arrayed across
laps or dull red seats where they sleep as

an exterior empty of light rumbles past.

2.
Truly, it's wonderful to slip into words
lit by a small bulb's light across a page.
And here comes a young man fully alert
(via the author) on a platform of snow.

Why is a mystery, the writer sleeping on it
beside a wife who, thank God, knows not
having a clue is what he's all about, and
that by and by it will come to him in a dream

filling five pages about, probably, a woman.

3.
Suddenly the scent of oranges permeates
the carriage as a very young Princess prepares
to eat from a basket sent by messenger from
her inescapably unsuitable suitor from whom

she has been told she must, alas, escape. And
now a greed beyond her breeding overtakes her
just as steam from the engine envelops wheels.
Isn't that just the way of unsuitable young men:

To satisfy appetite until it feels like love?

4.
Refuse! Refuse! whispers Princess to all the
construction others demand of her. Well!
Reader says to herself midway through a
journey begun, admittedly, against all advice.

Is this not my very own life of such un-
certain splendor I doubted the arrogance
of a reserved seat? And why must history
always turn plums into prunes? But we

must not, Reader, switch fruits, so she turns

5.
the page and again steps into her paginated life
wherein Princess departs the train and, most
naturally, lifts both arms as the now entirely
suitably suitor whirls her wildly around: Oh!

Reason simply can't compete. And what
happens next to Reader predates literature
itself and she will report none of it: No!
Except of course: Oranges are delicious

especially eaten by Him and Her in bed.

# WOMAN ON A BENCH

To be told you will die of an illness
in two seasons, not, it goes without

saying, of your choosing, is to find an
animosity toward lovers furiously

turning the spit of time on straw beds
bound in cotton ticking; a village

where the baker burned the brioche
after his wife ran off with the mason.

What went on inside his house afterwards?
Some delicate, slow-rising guilt for all the

recent disasters of insufficient yeast? And
does this merit the telling, when, so we

are led to believe, the baker drove her mad?
She went. His brioche, especially the ones

studded with raisins or hidden pillows of
chocolate, looked almost normal again, if

a bit salty. . . . All of this drama consumed
less time than you can imagine, so many

pages given over to the mason and the wife
touring the French countryside. That was

insipid, not my cup of tea at all in my current
state. I shall, in fact, give up all novels of

romance, espionage, and murder. As soon as
I decide when to die.

# VERGING ON EXTINCTION

We know it is time to leave, yet
    here we are, nervous

and restive. Eyes so opaque on an
    earth swollen with

and despoiled by us. Pulse-beats
    out in space, hoar frost

of stars invade our bodies old enough
    to connect that chill

and the artificial coolness of houses
    where children whimper.

In answer to what might yet become
    a contagion of suffocation,

we contemplate seizures of terror
    stretching the mouths of

whomever receives us from the once
    flower-scented place those many

wounds ago when we were cherished.

# Some Previous Titles in the Carnegie Mellon Poetry Series

2013
*Oregon*, Henry Carlile
*Selvage*, Donna Johnson
*At the Autopsy of Vaslav Nijinksy*, Bridget Lowe
*Silvertone*, Dzivinia Orlowsky
*Fibonacci Batman: New & Selected Poems*, Maureen Seaton
*When We Were Cherished*, Eve Shelnutt
*The Fortunate Era*, Arthur Smith
*Birds of the Air*, David Yezzi

2012
*Now Make an Altar*, Amy Beeder
*Still Some Cake*, James Cummins
*Comet Scar*, James Harms
*Early Creatures, Native Gods*, K. A. Hays
*That Was Oasis*, Michael McFee
*Blue Rust*, Joseph Millar
*Spitshine*, Anne Marie Rooney
*Civil Twilight*, Margot Schilpp

2011
*Having a Little Talk with Capital P Poetry*, Jim Daniels
*Oz*, Nancy Eimers
*Working in Flour*, Jeff Friedman
*Scorpio Rising: Selected Poems*, Richard Katrovas
*The Politics*, Benjamin Paloff
*Copperhead*, Rachel Richardson

2010
*The Diminishing House*, Nicky Beer
*A World Remembered*, T. Alan Broughton
*Say Sand*, Daniel Coudriet
*Knock Knock*, Heather Hartley
*In the Land We Imagined Ourselves*, Jonathan Johnson

*Selected Early Poems: 1958-1983*, Greg Kuzma
*The Other Life: Selected Poems*, Herbert Scott
*Admission*, Jerry Williams

2009
*Divine Margins*, Peter Cooley
*Cultural Studies*, Kevin A. González
*Dear Apocalypse*, K. A. Hays
*Warhol-o-rama*, Peter Oresick
*Cave of the Yellow Volkswagen*, Maureen Seaton
*Group Portrait from Hell*, David Schloss
*Birdwatching in Wartime*, Jeffrey Thomson

2008
*The Grace of Necessity*, Samuel Green
*After West*, James Harms
*Anticipate the Coming Reservoir*, John Hoppenthaler
*Convertible Night, Flurry of Stones*, Dzvinia Orlowsky
*Parable Hunter*, Ricardo Pau-Llosa
*The Book of Sleep*, Eleanor Stanford

2007
*Trick Pear*, Suzanne Cleary
*So I Will Till the Ground*, Gregory Djanikian
*Black Threads*, Jeff Friedman
*Drift and Pulse*, Kathleen Halme
*The Playhouse Near Dark*, Elizabeth Holmes
*On the Vanishing of Large Creatures*, Susan Hutton
*One Season Behind*, Sarah Rosenblatt
*Indeed I Was Pleased with the World*, Mary Ruefle
*The Situation*, John Skoyles

2006
*Burn the Field*, Amy Beeder
*The Sadness of Others*, Hayan Charara
*A Grammar to Waking*, Nancy Eimers
*Dog Star Delicatessen: New and Selected Poems*, Mekeel McBride
*Shinemaster*, Michael McFee

*Eastern Mountain Time*, Joyce Peseroff
*Dragging the Lake*, Robert Thomas

2005
*Things I Can't Tell You*, Michael Dennis Browne
*Bent to the Earth*, Blas Manuel De Luna
*Blindsight*, Carol Hamilton
*Fallen from a Chariot*, Kevin Prufer
*Needlegrass*, Dennis Sampson
*Laws of My Nature*, Margot Schilpp
*Sleeping Woman*, Herbert Scott
*Renovation*, Jeffrey Thomson

2004
*The Women Who Loved Elvis All Their Lives*, Fleda Brown
*The Chronic Liar Buys a Canary*, Elizabeth Edwards
*Freeways and Aqueducts*, James Harms
*Prague Winter*, Richard Katrovas
*Trains in Winter*, Jay Meek
*Tristimania*, Mary Ruefle
*Venus Examines Her Breast*, Maureen Seaton
*Various Orbits*, Thom Ward

2003
*Trouble*, Mary Baine Campbell
*A Place Made of Starlight*, Peter Cooley
*Taking Down the Angel*, Jeff Friedman
*Lives of Water*, John Hoppenthaler
*Imitation of Life*, Allison Joseph
*Except for One Obscene Brushstroke*, Dzvinia Orlowsky
*The Mastery Impulse*, Ricardo Pau-Llosa
*Casino of the Sun*, Jerry Williams

2002
*Keeping Time*, Suzanne Cleary
*Astronaut*, Brian Henry
*What it Wasn't*, Laura Kasischke
*Slow Risen Among the Smoke Trees*, Elizabeth Kirschner

*The Finger Bone*, Kevin Prufer
*Among the Musk Ox People*, Mary Ruefle
*The Late World*, Arthur Smith

2001
*Day Moon*, Jon Anderson
*The Origin of Green*, T. Alan Broughton
*Lovers in the Used World*, Gillian Conoley
*Quarters*, James Harms
*Mastodon, 80% Complete*, Jonathan Johnson
*The Deepest Part of the River*, Mekeel McBride
*Earthly*, Michael McFee
*Ten Thousand Good Mornings*, James Reiss
*The World's Last Night*, Margot Schilpp
*Sex Lives of the Poor and Obscure*, David Schloss
*Glacier Wine*, Maura Stanton
*Voyages in English*, Dara Wier

2000
*Blue Jesus*, Jim Daniels
*Years Later*, Gregory Djanikian
*Winter Morning Walks: 100 Postcards to Jim Harrison*, Ted Kooser
*Mortal Education*, Joyce Peseroff
*How Things Are*, James Richardson
*On the Waterbed They Sank to Their Own Levels*, Sarah Rosenblatt
*Post Meridian*, Mary Ruefle
*Constant Longing*, Dennis Sampson
*Hierarchies of Rue*, Roger Sauls
*Small Boat with Oars of Different Size*, Thom Ward